Psychic Development

A Complete Guide to Awakening Your Third Eye and Developing Your Psychic Abilities

Jamie Parr

Table of Contents

Introduction 1

Chapter 1: What Are the Different Psychic Abilities 3

Chapter 2: What Is the Third Eye 17

Chapter 3: How to Awaken the Third Eye 24

Chapter 4: How to View Auras 38

Chapter 5: Clairvoyance 49

Chapter 6: Telepathy 56

Chapter 7: How to Develop the Different Psychic Abilities 63

Conclusion 69

Introduction

I sincerely congratulate you for purchasing *Psychic Development,* and I have the utmost gratitude that you have done so. Thank you for choosing to venture with me into the realm of psychic understanding.

Psychic abilities are around us every day. From the woman standing before you in the check out line, to your next-door neighbor, to your partner sitting right next to you, to you yourself. There is so much untapped psychic potential within each and every one of us. You just have to learn how to reach out, grab it, hold it close, and make it your own. I strive to help you do that in this very book.

If you trust me to do so, I wish to guide you on this mystical path through uncharted spiritual territory. With this book by your side or in your hands, you can unlock abilities within yourself that you may not have even known existed. Let me open your eyes, all three of them, and show you just what you can do if you give yourself the chance.

I fully believe that everyone can hone their psychic abilities. Whether one or many abilities call out to you, I want to help you hear the call and act on it. I know that everyone can do this if they put their mind and their heart into it. It can benefit you and many others if you do. I trust that you will take this to heart and blossom into the psychic being you were destined to become.

In your journey through this book, we will discuss and learn about the awakening of your third eye, which is present in us all. We will also thoroughly confer about your innermost psychic abilities and how to develop them further. I will go over a plethora of psychic abilities discovered throughout the millennia, and I will give the most detailed overview of each so you can hyper focus on those which call out to you.

Then, I will carefully guide you through the process of discovering your own abilities, honing them, and developing them so that you may utilize them throughout your lifespan. If you do so, your eyes will be opened to many wondrous things!

Among the topics discussed will be the third eye and its awakening, the six clair senses with a focus on clairvoyance, seeking out and identifying auras, telepathy and reading signs from other beings, and much more!

As you may well know, many like-minded authors have published similar books about psychic abilities and the third eye, and I am gracious to you for choosing mine out of the books available. Every effort was made to give you the most structured guide possible, full of as much spiritual clarity as I could muster. I assure you that the content within this book is full of rich, useful information for your spiritual journey. I hope you enjoy reading it!

Chapter 1: What Are the Different Psychic Abilities

There are many psychic abilities swirling around us every day that are untapped or unrecognized. Let's go over some of the most common psychic abilities that we can experience so you can see which one, or ones, you may identify with!

Awakening the Third Eye

Awakening the third eye is any person's first step to unlocking their psychic abilities. It is a psychic ability within itself because it unlocks the ease and ability to access and identify the other abilities within oneself. It is, arguably, the most important ability for anyone to have who wishes to utilize their psychic abilities.

Meditation

Meditation is key to centering oneself and finding true balance. It allows you to quiet the turmoil of the world and focus solely on your senses and abilities in the psychic realm. It is not only beneficial to your abilities, but it is beneficial to you as a whole. It calms your body, your mind, and your spirit. It is a wonderful ability to practice in order to enlighten yourself and aid your mind in identifying everything in the spiritual realm. Meditation helps with all other psychic abilities, and it helps one hyper focus on their senses and the realms of interaction around them. It is also very healing, and it ties in quite closely with the spiritual forms of healing we will talk about soon.

Aura Viewing and Reading

Auras are present in every living thing. It is believed that they are created out of an electromagnetic field around a living being's very body, and it is an indication of their negative, positive, or neutral energy. They are often identified by colors, patterns, and/or vibrations. Each of these is specially designated to the entity with which it resides and surrounds.

When one can identify and connect an aura to a physical or spiritual body, he or she can determine the character and energy of the being that the aura embodies. Each aura is unique to its physical or spiritual counterpart and tells the story of who they are inside, to some extent.

The Six Clair Senses

There are six psychic senses that are often referred to as the six clair senses. They go beyond our natural, worldly senses and expand our third eye so we can reach into the ether and extrapolate clear ideas of the psychic realm around us and within us. The most common of these, and the one I will be focusing on primarily in this book, is clairvoyance. However, I will go over each of them in detail so you can get a full, true understanding of these wonderful abilities we can all find within ourselves.

Clairvoyance

Clairvoyance is the most popular, arguably, of the six clair senses. This clair sense has to do with seeing, either with your physical eyes or your awakened third eye, images, entities, passed loved ones, spirit guides, animals, mental images, clips of events like a video, flashes of pictures, and/or strange writing and visual messages. Through direct translation from the French language, Clairvoyance means clear vision. This is because you visually, either with your physical eyes or third eye, see things with such clarity you can't miss them unless you are in denial or have not recognized or developed your clairvoyant ability. Clairvoyance is closely linked to the sixth chakra, also known as the Ajna, or Third Eye chakra.

Clairaudience

Clairaudience is defined by the ability to hear spirits through thoughts, music, sounds pertaining to nature, through a possession, via a medium, or whilst touching an inanimate object that is linked to the paranormal realm. It is a sense that only those in tune with their clair abilities can hear. These sounds are often inaudible to those around the individual with the psychic connection to the sound. Clairaudience is linked to the fifth chakra, also known as the Vishuddha, or throat chakra.

Clairsentience

Clairsentience is attributed most closely to the human sense of feeling. It is deeper than physical touch, however, and ties more familiarly with internal feelings or musings. With this clair sense, one can deduce facts about a person, even a stranger, that they would never have been able to discover elsewhere. For example, one with clairsentience might know the name of a stranger as they enter the room before that individual has had the chance to introduce themselves. Many people with this psychic ability use it to open up some type of fortune telling business. Some use it to help out detectives, if those individuals accept their psychic abilities. It is one of the most intimate psychic abilities and can be shocking to people unfamiliar to this clair sense. This is because it can, at times, make people uncomfortable when their information, such as their date of birth, zodiac sign, or occupation, are revealed by a complete stranger. Clairsentience is linked to the second chakra, also known as the Svadhisthana, or sacral chakra.

Clairalience

Clairalience is linked to the physical sense of smell. This is a very common psychic ability in people, though they may not realize it. Let me give an example. A woman, whose father had passed many years prior, smells the cologne of her father at a precious family event, such as a birth. There is no way that smell could have entered the room, as no environmental factors had changed. It is probable that this woman experienced clairalience by smelling a familiar scent from her father from the spiritual realm. More often than not, the individual with an attunement to clairalience is the only one who notices this scent, as the individual is likely linked to them in a precious or specific way.

Clairgustance

Clairgustance is very similar to clairalience, but it targets a person's sense of taste. With this clair sense, you can taste material without that particular substance being within physical reach of your tongue and taste buds. Instead of tasting the actual food, you taste its energy, however. It can even be that which is not in the food category. You could taste the sweetness of water, cool wind, bitter flowers, the rough bark of a tree, rich soil, specific places, people, yourself, and other natural or unnatural entities. You can even taste the energies of thoughts, feelings, and possibly memories. This sense can be jarring, and it is not always pleasant. A sudden, nasty taste in your mouth when you are not around anything remotely similar to the taste, can be a form of clairgustance. Similarly, the taste of a favorite fruit a loved one used to enjoy can be a faint clairgustance of a memory. These tastes can be, and often are, closely tied to the feelings of those around you. If someone is experiencing bad health, you may taste something sour, or if someone is having a joyous day, you could taste something sweet.

Claircognizance

Claircognizance is what most people refer to as the sixth sense. There have been movies based on this clair sense, though this ability is far from fictional. This clair sense goes beyond the familiar human senses into a primal, instinctual feeling. In the mildest of occurrences, this can be as simple as the hair standing on the back of your neck when you sense someone entering a room. When you turn around and notice a figure behind you, you realize that this gut sense is correct. It is also the clair sense that is linked to discernment, and those with this sense are very skilled at detecting liars. However, it is most often attributed to being able to gain the impression of the presence of a supernatural being, or a spirit, in the area in which you sense their existence. Claircognizance is linked to the seventh chakra, also known as the Sahasrara, or crown chakra.

Telepathy

Telepathy is a psychic ability that most skeptics laugh at. It is very real, my friends. Telepathy is the ability to hear the innermost thoughts and/or feelings of others, read the mind of an individual or individuals, or transmit thoughts, feelings, and information to another person without visual or auditory means. It is a rich form of psychic communication, and it is often sorely untapped.

In modern society, a common reference to telepathy would be that of a hivemind, which means that a group of individuals share the same thought processes, knowledge, commands, or feelings within or between one another. Hivemind can have other applications outside the psychic dominion, but it is very much present in this discipline. You can hone it and use it among friends and family, if you so desire. It is best, however, to do so with their consent.

There are many forms of telepathy, each of which I will detail later in this book in the chapter dedicated specifically to telepathy. These forms include latent telepathy, retrocognitive telepathy, precognitive telepathy, intuitive telepathy, emotive telepathy, and superconscious telepathy.

Hypnosis

Hypnosis is a psychic ability that has many practical uses in our society today. Many verify its importance, and quite a few psychics and therapists alike use it to unlock feelings, memories, and information in their clients. Hypnosis uses a sleep-like state to unlock hidden truths and a wide expanse of feelings, memories, and emotions in an individual. It is very helpful, and it can be used primarily for good. It is safest, however, to always have more than one person in the room when hypnosis occurs in order for the individual under its effects to feel safe and secure.

By definition, hypnosis occurs when you are in a very calm, intensely focused state of mind. The feeling of sleepiness, or the out of body experience that is applied under the hypnotic state, helps the mind to concentrate on unlocked potential that can come in many forms. It lessens peripheral awareness and distractions, allowing your mind and body to become fully at peace so that your walls lower and allow the mind's vulnerability to unleash emotions, memories, thoughts, and information that can be incredibly beneficial to you or the individual involved.

Hypnosis can be misinterpreted as meditation, but while they are very similar states of mind, they are not one and the same. Meditation is self-induced, and the individual that is meditating is in full control and fully self-aware. With hypnosis, it is often induced by a separate person, and the individual under hypnosis is not self-aware. In fact, the hypnotized individual is usually in a trance, under a state of amnesia, or completely unconscious.

Healing

There are many forms of psychic healing, from internal healing through proper meditation and balance, to energy and physical healings. I will go over some of the most recognizable forms here in detail so you can further your journey into the realm of psychic healing. These are just a few examples, as there are many more, but I would like to focus on these for the time being. Included will be both hands on and hands-off approaches to psychic healing.

Crystals

Crystals give us a very physical and intimate connection to earthly and spiritual energies. These energies can be used for good and bad, but we are going to focus on the positive energies emitted from crystals because these are the ones that contribute to an individual's healing. Common healing crystals include emeralds, black obsidian, carnelians, rose quartz, and the master healer, clear quartz. All of these crystals, and more, have wonderful healing capabilities for the mind, body, and soul. They cleanse negative energy from the air, uplift your spirit, heal the body, and ground and center the mind's turmoil. There is a lot of raw healing power in crystals if you choose to pursue them.

Acupuncture

Many people cringe at the thought of acupuncture, but it genuinely has incredibly beneficial healing properties for the body. Acupuncture is just as spiritual as it is physical, as it targets pressure points as well as chakras. Acupuncture balances your chakra at specific points in the body, releasing negative energies and allowing positive ones to flow in. It also utilizes thin, harmless needles to relieve bodily strain at pressure points. Your energy stores will be wonderfully balanced if you choose to use acupuncture as a healing modality.

Reiki

Reiki is a wonderful way to balance and restore equilibrium to your Third Eye chakra. Through this form of energy healing, your spirit and body will purify and become quite at peace. By means of physical touch by another person, your body will awaken, and the positive energy will activate healing processes within your entire body. Your physical and emotional wellness will be substantially improved through these means as long as a true believer who has honed his or her abilities is administering this therapy to you correctly. This Japanese-originated healing process is a wonderful way to reduce stress and tension in the body and mind.

Tai Chi

Tai Chi is an ancient Chinese practice that internalizes energies and uses the body's fists to create an equilibrium with the polarities known as Yin and Yang. This balancing art symbolizes the fusion of two opposites into a complete, ultimate energy to boost internal defense and strength. This practice is often used in martial arts, but it can also be easily applied to the art of psychic abilities. Balancing energies and creating equilibrium within one's being can aid in healing the defenses of the mind and body, safeguarding them from negative energies and attacks.

Qigong

Qigong is similar to Tai Chi, but it is more fluidly practiced in order to combine breathing, posture, movement, and meditation into a healing rhythm that benefits the spirit, health, and discipline of the body and mind. This practice can help develop psychic disciplines and make it easier to tune into your many senses as well as surrounding energies.

Extrasensory Perception (ESP)

Extrasensory Perception, or ESP, involves a person's ability to sense, read, and determine supernatural presences through the detection of electromagnetic fields and energies. This ability is actually a branch of the sixth sense, claircognizance. Specifically, however, it targets the reception of images, supernatural beings, information, and more entirely through the mind and instinctual senses, instead of the physical senses. It has also been referred to as second sight. It can also incorporate other psychic abilities, including precognition and remote viewing, which we will discuss further in the next sections of this chapter.

Remote Viewing

Remote viewing is a specific psychic ability that channels ESP to search for and find impressions of a target that cannot be seen with the physical eyes, or from an individual's current physical position. It is called remote viewing because things are seen in remote or distant locations within the physical or spiritual realm. Through remote viewing, one can collect information about a person, place, or occurrence that is far away without having to utilize or tap into all of your clair senses. These images normally come in bits and pieces and are not normally fluid.

Retrocognition and Precognition

Retrocognition and precognition are psychic abilities that often intertwine and work hand in hand. They allow a psychic individual to gather information about events that occurred in the past, as well as to gain a sense of what will happen in the future.

Retrocognition

Retrocognition pertains to seeing past events without the use of one's own memory. They see clips or snippets of the past that could not have been attained otherwise, except through the mind's eye and the spiritual realm.

Precognition

Precognition is the psychic ability that pertains to foreseeing the future. It is also referred to as prescience. Precognition typically uses claircognizance and/or visions and thoughts to predict what the future holds. Psychic practitioners will often combine their sense of precognition with information obtained through retrocognition to more accurately predict what is to come.

Psychometry

Psychometry involves a person touching certain objects in order to feel the presence of a previous owner, thus learning the item's history and the story behind that object and/or the person connected with it.

Automatic Writing

This psychic ability is important enough to be mentioned in detail, but this is the only time it will be mentioned in this book, as it is an ability that cannot normally be controlled. Therefore, it cannot be controlled and developed, so we cannot discuss its development in detail in this book. With that said, this psychic ability is best defined as the ability for writing to be scripted through the channeling of another person, or the ability to write on a surface with one's subconscious, without being aware of the action. This inability to be aware of the writing itself is why it is generally considered to be uncontrollable.

Chapter 2: What Is the Third Eye

The Third Eye is an eye that is not physical. We cannot see it with our eyes of flesh, but it is omnipresent. The Third Eye is what most call the mind's eye. It is the eye with which we view visions, see the psychic realm, and experience clairvoyance. Opening the mind's eye is the first step to awakening our psychic abilities. In this chapter, I will go over what the mind's eye is, its origins as we know them in history, and its application throughout history.

What Is the Third Eye?

The Third Eye represents the phenomenon that occurs when your internal energies and psychic affiliations reach a peak within your mind, creating an opening in your mind through which you can sense the psychic realm of understanding. Your overall vision and reception to spiritual existence reaches a heightened point of clarity through which you can begin meditating and developing your abilities to awaken your own psychic channels and abilities. You also gain a new, unique understanding of life, dimensions, supernatural senses, and so much more.

It is an awakening, of sorts, once you tap into your mind's eye. You can see the world, and life, beyond the normal realms of understanding and the basic limitations of your physical body's perceptive abilities. This perception, with the mind's eye, rises, or awakens, beyond the physical plane of being. It has also been known to allow people to achieve cosmic vision.

Once you awaken your third eye, you can begin developing your psychic abilities. Among those are the six clair senses. While the sixth clair sense has often been referred to as one's sixth sense, the Third Eye has also been commonly called the sixth sense, as it awakens those abilities, among others. That is because it gives us a heightened sense of different dimensions around us that cannot be experienced with our five physical senses.

Where Is the Third Eye?

The Third Eye is not an eye that represents itself in a physical way. This is why many call it the mind's eye. In artwork, it is depicted as being located on a person's forehead, representing the eye emanating from within the brain. It is an inner eye that you can turn inward or outward to discover new mystical experiences within yourself, or to experience new things while surveying the universe around you. Your physical eyes can only see what is right in front of you, turning outside to your environment. The mind's eye can see so much more in so many different dimensions.

Another reason, other than that the brain is behind your forehead, for the third eye to be represented at that location, is that the sixth dimension's chakra is located above the point on your face where your eyebrows meet. The Third Eye's placement represents this chakra and its capabilities when paired with the mind's eye. Depending on the movement of energy within your body, the Third Eye will help you awaken different capabilities within your own life, be it pleasure, drive, necessities, or certain jobs and skills. The most achievable capability you can develop through the Third Eye is your clarity of vision, particularly with your clairvoyance. It gives you the ability to see things clearly in your life, though not necessarily the experience you need. That comes with practice and through experiencing all of life's challenges.

The Origins of the Third Eye

The Third Eye is said to have originated from Shiva, who is portrayed in ancient stories as being able to open this Third Eye and access an omniscient channel of psychic sight. The Third Eye's placement, and the sixth dimension's chakra, are attached to three dimensions that represent and are named after the three different forms of Shiva. They are three points at which we experience different phenomenon in the body. When your energy moves to one of those points it can alter your understanding and perception of life itself.

This origin story of the Third Eye is the most accepted, and comes from deep-rooted spiritual traditions in the Indian culture. These traditions are Dharmic in nature and point to the Third Eye as the brow, or in their language the Ajna, chakra. This chakra directs a person's energy into the Third Eye, allowing it to open up a floodgate into mystical realms and dimensions. Through this awakening of the Third Eye, a person can unlock a higher realm of knowing or a higher consciousness. This consciousness is near-godly in nature, making it almost omniscient.

The term "Third Eye" as we know it was actually coined in English in the 1800s. As the Indian culture referred to it as the Ajna chakra and not an actual Third Eye, those who spoke the English language named it so to give it a more visual name. In the later 1800s, it was further defined by a Russian occult woman, Helena Blavatsky, as the capability of inner vision outside the realm of physical possibility. She believed that this ability originated from the ancestors of humanity itself.

Regardless of the origin of the Third Eye, it has been intertwined with history and humanity for generations. It all comes down to balance, awakening, and a higher level of knowledge. Next, we will go over where the Third Eye has shown up in human history and literature.

The Third Eye Throughout History and Literature

Throughout history, the Third Eye has symbolized enlightenment and higher knowledge. Specifically, it has been present in the same circles as auras and chakras, precognition, and experiences that happen out of one's own body. These instances have been charted and recorded throughout the years, and though the Third Eye itself is older than the written word, I will now share some of the most famous instances of the Third Eye chakra awakening throughout time in segments of history and literature alike.

The Third Eye in Human History

- Hindu Puranas from the fourth century onward recount instances of the Third Eye in sacred Sanskrit writings, folklore, and legends. The most notable Third Eye in this culture is the Third Eye of the god Shiva. Other Hindu deities with a Third Eye include Daksha, Ganesha, Brahma, Durga, and Kali.

- Ingebord Refling Hagen, a Norwegian author, stated in her Magnum Opus that she had an internal mentor she referred to as "the old one," who appeared in her mind as a single grey eye. She noted that she gained insight through this eye, and it could very well be a reference to the Third Eye.

- In the Chinese culture, there is a deity named Er Lang Shen, who is said to have a Third Eye that allows him to see through deceit and disguise.

- In the 1960s, in Japan, a scholar of Zen Buddhism named Daisetz Teitaro Suzuki, delineated the Third Eye as one's ability to overcome ignorance.

- Throughout history and in the modern day, the Third Eye has been used in conjunction with the practice of doing yoga. Yogis throughout the New Age movement have used it to help their students tune in to their chakras and unlock the potential of their spiritual vision.

- Much more modern than the other accounts of the Third Eye, comedian Bill Hicks has been recorded stating that he believed his Third Eye to have opened after taking certain drugs that made him hallucinate. He used this as more of a metaphor, but it is relevant to the instance of the Third Eye being referenced in modern, popular culture. It goes hand in hand with a 1966 article called "LSD and the Third Eye," which links psychedelic drugs to chakras and the awakening of new circumstances of consciousness.

The Third Eye in Literature

- In 1959, Lobsang Rampa wrote the fictional novel titled *The Third Eye,* which introduced the concept of the third eye to a large audience for the first time in the English popular reading culture.

- In the literature of Greek Mythology, the cyclops referenced in the *Odyssey* has been linked to the Third Eye. He sees with a singular perspective, and though he does not have three eyes, or even two, he has been compared to the concept of the Third Eye. However, throughout folklore and oral traditions, many depictions of the cyclops have shown him having three eyes.

Chapter 3: How to Awaken the Third Eye

In this chapter, we will cover how to awaken the Third Eye, develop it, and hone its abilities. This step-by-step guide will aid you in unlocking the unmatched psychic potential that you will be able to carry with you through your entire life, if you so choose. By fully awakening your Third Eye, your health and outlook on life will be so much greater, and your ability to achieve your psychic potential will be exponentially better. This is because you will be intellectually realized, and nothing can disturb you or take as big of a toll on you because you are so much more aware and awakened to the universe around you, and its energies. It will give you stability and balance in life, or an equilibrium, to the point that it feels like nothing can worry you. Let's now discover how to turn your Third Eye inward and fully awaken its potential!

Chakras

To begin, we will talk about chakras. Chakras are like wheels, or spinning vortexes, of energy within your body. Each wheel, so to speak, constantly moves and influences the energies in specific points of your body. Proper knowledge of chakras is imperative to awakening the mind's eye, which is directly linked to the third eye chakra itself. Chakras are specific points within oneself that host your internal energy stores. How you direct that energy affects your psychic abilities, health, and much more. Chakras are linked to the endocrine system, in fact, and your ability to balance your chakras will aid you with many of the body's processes. Specifically, your hormone levels can improve with proper understanding and cleansing of your chakras. Learning to direct your energy from the other six of your chakras to Ajna, the third eye chakra, is the first step to awakening your mind's eye. Here, we will learn about each of the seven chakras before we focus on the third eye chakra specifically.

1. **The Root Chakra (Muladhara)** – This chakra is the rooting point of our energy. With this chakra, we can strengthen our entire body and mind if we utilize it correctly. It is located at the very base of our spine, and it controls the primal urges of sleep, sexual intercourse and desire, hunger and satiation, and self-preservation. It is connected to the element of the earth, as that is where we root ourselves in this plane of existence. We gain strength and stability with this chakra, which helps us to maintain balance and posture.

2. **The Sacral Chakra (Svadhisthana)** – This chakra is located in our pelvis, and it flows through you like the water that it has an affinity toward. It controls our sexual energy, fluidity, ability to adapt to situations, creativity and imagination, feelings, and our unconscious thoughts

and desires. It helps us regulate our emotions and our innermost desires so that they do not control us. It helps us access our untapped creative potential as well.

3. **The Navel Chakra (Manipura)** – This chakra is located in the center of our navel. It burns with the power of fire, and it helps us digest and understand our desires, our experiences in life, and the food we eat. It gives us the power to walk through the different stages of our lives, and heightens our innermost strength and our determination. It gives us confidence and drive. It helps us overcome life's obstacles and struggles.

4. **The Heart Chakra (Anahata)** – This precious chakra coincides with the wind and resides in the center of our hearts. It gives us a nearly indestructible spiritual high that allows us to rise above life's pains and burdens. It helps us develop peace, feel love, and have an open mind. It is arguably the most spiritual of the chakras in the sense that it connects with our very souls. It is also very emotional, and it gives us the gift of unconditional love.

5. **The Throat Chakra (Vishuddha)** – This chakra, located at the base of our throat, gives us our voice. It allows us to speak out and lace truth into our lives. It is an ethereal chakra that has no physical ties, but rather a tie to space itself and the element of the very ether of the universe. It allows us to define ourselves and find our unique forms of self-expression and independence. It gives us the power to live in a world of truth and to speak the truth once we tap into it.

6. **The Third Eye Chakra (Ajna)** – This chakra is the one we will be focusing on primarily in this chapter. It is the chakra directly linked to your Third Eye, and it is the chakra we will be channeling our energy into so that we may awaken its potential. The Ajna chakra is located right above the point where our eyebrows meet, which is where the Third Eye is depicted in ancient cultures and art. It is where our mind resides, as well as both our subconscious and conscious forms of awareness. It has no elemental affinity, as it reaches beyond the realm of common understandings and the elements of the earth and physical means. This is the chakra of true vision, primal intuition and instinct, prophecy and divination, true imagination, dreams, self-assurance, and spirituality. It gives us the greatest insight into ourselves and the universe once we truly awaken its potential power. It gives

us great knowledge of our own emotions, mentality, and spiritual existence. It is the most open of the chakras once it is unlocked and awakened. It is also the chakra most closely linked to the art of meditation.

7. **The Crown Chakra (Sahasrara)** – This chakra is located at the highest point of our head or our crown. Much like the third eye chakra, it is beyond elemental ties. It is the gateway to the purest form of consciousness and is our way of reaching our highest point of self. It is also a way to connect directly to divine springs of energy. It gives us true enlightenment, mastery of self, and an untapped connection to all that is in the universe and beyond. It, too, is closely linked to the divine practice of meditation. This chakra allows us to surrender ourselves to an enlightened state of mind and pure consciousness. It also opens doors for our inspirations.

How to Awaken the Third Eye

Let us awaken our sixth sense now, and find the true meaning of the Third Eye's unveiled power. Follow the steps below to fully awaken your mind's eye.

Fill Your Surroundings with Sixth Chakra Colors

Your Ajna chakra is closely tied to the color indigo. By wearing this color, along with blues and purples, and decorating your space with them, you can become more in tune with your Third Eye's chakra. The sixth chakra's energies will flow out and embrace these colors, connecting you in a more visual way to its energy. You can wear jewelry with precious stones in these colors, fill your home with healing crystals, and wear clothing in these colors to bring yourself closer to your Ajna chakra in an intimate way.

Consume Sixth Chakra Colors

Much like wearing the colors associated with the Third Eye, eating foods in the same range of color will allow your body to become more in-tune with your Ajna chakra. These foodswill impregnate your body with sixth chakra energies:

- Blueberries
- Beets
- Blackberries
- Eggplants
- Red Grapes
- Prunes

Fill the Room With Fragrance

Burn incense, use essential oils, or bathe with the following scents to imbue your body with aromas that will help activate your sixth chakra:

- Nutmeg
- Grapefruit
- Sandalwood
- Chamomile
- Myrrh

Meditate

Breathe. Calm your body, calm your mind, calm your soul. Breathe in and out, focus your mind on the energy flowing through your chakras, and open your palms to the sky. Let yourself relax and give in to your senses, hyper focusing on all that is inside of you while keeping distractions at bay. Get comfortable, unwind, and open yourself up to your feelings, thoughts, and more while letting your mind flow outside of the realm of your very body.

Open and Heal the Body's Energy Centers With Yoga

Yoga is one of the body's greatest ways to stay in tune with your chakras. It focuses and practices your breathing, your focus, your strength and determination, your flexibility, and more, all of which are useful when awakening your Third Eye. Yoga will cleanse your body and your energies while balancing your chakras and your physical form. These yoga poses are among the best for strengthening and opening your mind's eye:

- Virasana (the Hero pose)
- Ardha Uttanasana (the Standing Half Forward Bend pose)
- Salamba Sarvangasana (the Supported Shoulderstand pose)
- Balasana (the Child's Pose)
- Adho Mukha Svanasana (the Downward-Facing Dog pose)

Make sure to do each of these poses safely, and only do poses that you are comfortable with performing. If you are unsure of how to perform these specific poses, choose familiar ones that may be easier for you or find a trusted yoga instructor to teach you how to unlock their full potential in a safe and calm environment.

Give in to Intuition

The Third Eye opens the door to true vision, insight, and advanced wisdom. In order to unlock this door, one must fully cultivate his or her intuition. Utilize one or more of these practices to unlock the potential power of your intuition and become closely linked to your Third Eye:

- Lucid Dream
- Read Tarot Cards
- Delve Into an Understanding of Horoscopes
- Explore New Ideas
- Let Loose
- Seek Knowledge of New Things
- Open Your Mind to New Spiritual Realms of Possibility
- Train Your Mind to Stop Being so Serious
- Research the Meaning to Your Dreams
- Get Curious About New Things
- Gain Confidence in Yourself
- Have Fun!

Break Down Barriers and Jubilate

Rejoice in your vitality and break down the blockers of your chakra energy. The best way to do this is to break free of bad habits, potential addictions that can enslave your mind and body, and exhaustion. Exercise, practice good health, eat well, and laugh! Find happiness and life in every way you can to unlock your free spirit and let only good vibes flow through. Negative vibes and energies can seriously hinder your mind's eye and all of your chakras in general. You can help yourself achieve this by eating healthy foods and filling your home with cleansing incense and positive healing crystals.

Let Your Mind Break Loose

Use your creative skills and allow your art, in whatever form it may be, to flow onto the canvas of your choice. This will unlock your sacral chakra and give your mind the flexibility it needs to break loose from rational thought and skepticism. Open up new gates to creative possibilities and allow your third eye to have more wiggle room to open into and burst into full bloom.

Utilize Your Root Chakra and Ground Yourself

Build up the foundations for your chakras so that when your mind's eye bursts open, you have a point of stability so that you do not unleash its energy into imperceptible channels. It will also allow you to open your Third Eye in a healthier way so that you can maintain it for longer and prevent negative symptoms of awakening the mind's eye. It will help you gain more clarity as well, for things will flow out in a more linear fashion, instead of in bits and pieces that can lead to confusion and frustration. If you are disoriented and have no grounds for balance, it will weaken your body's ability to handle your Third Eye.

Grounding yourself can also help you unleash your Third Eye in a safe, gradual manner with your feet planted safely on the ground. If you are impatient and unlock your Third Eye prematurely, it can be very dangerous, and you could spiral out of control. Make sure you have a very stable foundation before you fully awaken your mind's eye so that you can have the greatest experience and the highest form of enlightenment that you can possibly achieve. Being grounded will also quell your fear when unfamiliar and unusual forms of energy get unleashed upon awakening your Third Eye.

How to Develop and Hone Your Third Eye

In addition to making the changes mentioned above, you will need to be diligent in practicing the following exercises and activites. These actions will support and reinforce your ability to maintain your Third Eye's awakening, and you will feel much more stable and comfortable if you utilize these means of fortification. Here is a list of ways to develop and strengthen your mind's eye:

- **Silent Meditation** – The key to this practice, and how it differs from other forms of meditation, is the absolute silence required to perform it. The silence allows you to fully focus on your chakras, energy, and perceptions of the world around you and that of the ethereal or spiritual realms.

- **Utilize the Moon** – Light from the moon has historically been an intimate source of intuition and spiritual awakening. Lay down under the light of the moon on calm nights and enter a state of reflection. This will fuel your center of intuition, which is key to maintaining the strength of your Third Eye.

- **Practice Divination** – This practice will help you tune in to the supernatural and the spiritual, and it will help you learn what to identify in your precognitions and retrocognitions once you awaken your mind's eye.

- **Let Your Imagination Run Wild** – Imagination opens up your mind and allows for previously undiscovered ideas and theories to spring forth and stomp skepticism into the ground. Skepticism will aid in the demise of your Third Eye's awakening, so it is best to take any measures possible to keep it away.

- **Lucid Dreaming** – Lucid dreaming, and dreaming in general, has been directly linked to your Third Eye. When you dream, you are in your deepest level of sleep. This is when the Third Eye is at its peak and comes out to play. By lucid dreaming, you can work with the Third Eye and control your dreamscape, thus unlocking a further understanding of your subconscious and your innermost intuitive capabilities.

- **Simply Exercise Your Intuitive Abilities** – This can be achieved in any means comfortable to you, but the intuition that resides in your mind is the primary function of your Third Eye.

- **Focus** – By this, I simply mean to close your eyes and train your mind to hear the quietest of whispers in the midst of silence. Your Third Eye, when it is first awakened, feels, and sounds much like a small whisper. You have to train yourself to identify what may have previously been imperceptible.

- **Strengthen Your Root and Throat Chakras** – Both of these chakras are pivotal anchors on which you balance the power of the unlocked Ajna's energies.

- **Get Curious and Study Symbolism** – Learn about different cultural symbols throughout time. This will open up your intuition and help you gain a wealth of knowledge that will allow you to better understand some of what you may learn and come into contact with once your Third Eye has awakened.

- **Read Between the Lines** – Learn to find inner and hidden meanings in words, phrases, ideas, and more so that your intuition can strengthen, and you can deduce meaning out of what may seem confusing.

Chapter 4: How to View Auras

Auras are surrounding each and every one of us. As you sit down, reading this book, you have an aura around you. The friends and family you see every day have their own auras around them. Even your pet has its own unique aura. They are all there, waiting to be discovered. Just because you have yet to see them does not mean they are not there. You just have to learn how to focus your psychic abilities, so you can view them as clear as you see the bright blue sky out your window. I am going to help you do just that. In this chapter, I will show you a step-by-step guide to heightening your psychic senses and viewing the auras around you. Honing your ability to view auras is a great step in your psychic development. In fact, it is a great first step for many who are trying to develop and hone their psychic abilities for the first time.

What Are Auras?

To begin, let's talk about what an aura is. We touched on this briefly in the first chapter of this book, but I will delve just a bit deeper here. An aura is an electromagnetic field that surrounds a living being. Each and every aura is special and unique to the person or being it surrounds. When you see them, they are visible as a color or colors, pattern or patterns, vibrations, or a combination of one or more of those aesthetics. What you see is an indication of who that person or being is at their core. It denotes negative, positive, and neutral energies. It will give you a good glimpse into what kind of person or being you are looking at. You can also get a small look into their story and their overall character. Auras never lie, so you will gain a wonderful understanding of a being's true personality when you learn to view and read auras.

Before we go into the next step, it important to note that auras have layers. Not only are there different colors of auras, but there are seven layers to these auras. Those layers are: Emotional, mental, etheric, etheric template, astral, celestial, and ketheric. These layers give a deep, rich understanding behind the meaning of auras and their different colors, patterns, and vibrations. The patterns can represent themselves in lines, shapes, swirls, or a variety of figures. Once you develop your psychic abilities properly, you will be well on your way to viewing all of these layers and gaining proper insight into what they all mean.

The etheric layer is closest to your body. It gives us the best indication of your physical health. If white spots show up on this layer, it could be an indication of health problems. The next layer that surrounds the etheric layer is the emotional layer. It reflects the feelings or emotions of an individual, and it is subject to change based on the mood of the individual. Dark spots on this layer indicate sadness or even depression. The next layer is the mental layer. This can indicate mental health and the mental state of an individual, as well as their beliefs and thoughts. Negative thoughts will be visible on this layer of the aura. The next layer is the astral layer, which acts as a hinge to connect the first three layers with the last three that I am about to describe. It is also a layer associated with an individual's very core, or heart, and the love that the individual feels. Next is the etheric template, which is also sometimes referred to as the manifestation layer. It is connected with an individual's capability of manifesting and creating things on a physical plane. Next is the celestial layer, and it is connected with your very spirit, spirituality, and overall intuition, which means it is likely the most closely linked aura layer to your mind's eye. It indicates an individual's level of higher consciousness and the individual's understanding of the world, universe, and the pure feeling of unconditional love. The final layer is the ketheric layer, the most spiritual of all of the layers. It is what connects us to the spiritual, divine, mystical, and the universe itself. It indicates one's connection to God or their deity of choice and their higher self as a whole. These seven layers combine into the complete aura of an individual, with each layer telling something different about that being.

How to View Auras: Step By Step

Reading auras is not difficult once you know what to do. In fact, it can take a matter of minutes once you get the hang of it!

Let's take this step by step:

1. Find a person to test this ability on with whom you are comfortable, or you can try it on yourself.

2. This step is just for if you are using yourself to practice on. If you are using yourself, go somewhere comfortable with a mirror, or look down at your hand and focus on that.

3. Once you have decided who you will practice on, place that person, or your hand, against either a completely dark background or a completely white one. This will make it easier to see the aura colors clearly. Black may be a bit easier, especially if the individual has a yellow, pink, or white aura.

4. Allow your subject, and/or yourself, a few moments to get perfectly relaxed.

5. Center yourself. Calm and still your mind, then find a balance in your surroundings. If you know how, focus your root chakra, or Muladhara, in order to ground yourself for stability purposes. Anchor your mind and body.

6. Take a deep breath and sense how the individual you are looking at makes you feel. Sense their energy so you can focus on it. That way, when you focus on that person, your mind will already be focusing on their energy.

7. Look straight at the individual, or your hand. Try to look at them out of focus. Looking from about seven or eight inches away from the individual helps with this. Try not to move any farther away than this, or you may not be able to sense the aura.

8. If you are looking at an individual and not your own hand, direct your attention to the area around the individual's

head. The strongest concentration of aura energies normally resides in this area.

9. Now, sit in complete silence and simply look and observe. This is why it is best to test on yourself or someone you are familiar with, as it can be a bit strange to stare at a stranger for too long. It may make that person uncomfortable.

10. Pay attention to and note any impressions, whether strong or faint, you may receive from your Third Eye, or Ajna. Its intuition is key here, for your mind's eye is the gateway for sensing these planes of psychic energy.

11. As you observe, you should at first see a thin white, possibly fuzzy line surrounding the head or body of the individual you are observing.

12. Then, once you see this white line, keep concentrating, and you should see the most prominent color or colors in the individual's aura.

13. Lastly, remember to be patient and maintain a completely open mind. Only then will you be able to truly view auras.

Over time, once you've practiced and mastered this psychic ability, you will begin to be able to view more and more layers of an individual's aura. Do not get discouraged! It just takes time and practice.

Practice, Practice, Practice!

At first, it may seem awkward to stare at people for a long time before viewing their auras. However, if you truly dedicate yourself and practice with something or someone more familiar, like a pet, spouse, sibling, or parent, it will begin to come much more naturally. In the beginning, it can take quite a bit of focusing in order to properly view an aura. However, once you have this skill under your belt, it can take minutes or even a single passing glance to view one's aura. You just have to practice! This is very important.

Once you practice enough, you may even be able to see more than just colors. You will be able to start identifying potential spots, patterns, and vibrations as well. You may also be able to view auras without the need for a solid background. This all comes with time and consistent practice.

How to Read Auras

Once we can clearly see auras, we need to know what they mean. Here, we will explain what many of the aura colors mean, what certain spots or inconsistencies mean, and more!

Colors

Aura layers often present themselves as colors. Here, we will discuss some commonly seen colors and what they may indicate:

- **Blue** – Blue is the color of an idealist. It also indicates an individual who closely follows principles, base morals, and overall ethics. These individuals are also often very intuitive, but can be prone to sensitivity.

- **Green** – Green is a beautiful color that resonates with the heart chakra or Anahata. It is the color of love, compassion, and loyalty. If an individual has this color, they are likely to be very trustworthy. Even further, if it is bright green, it indicates a very open heart full of acceptance. However, if it is a muddy green color, a bit darker than the positive light green, then it may indicate jealousy, insecurity, or a victim mentality.

- **Red** – Red is a strong color. It embodies empowerment and leadership. It also indicates an individual who is very brave in the face of fear or adversity. However, this color is often linked to someone who is quick to anger.

- **Pink** – Pink is a soft color that is very dear. Those with a pink aura are normally very loving and affectionate, try to keep the peace, wholeheartedly care for others, and are very good at mediating and being diplomatic.

- **Yellow** – Yellow is a bubbly color. It indicates high energy or liveliness, as well as a solid communicative ability, high intelligence, and the ability of that individual to be a good teacher or mentor. Normally, individuals with this color are playful and fun.

- **Orange** – Orange is a very fluid color. It indicates one's ability to open up their imaginations. Those with an orange aura are likely to be very creative, independent, and self-confident. Those with this aura are also generally very adventurous and productive.

- **Purple** – Purple is a very rich color. It is closely linked to the spiritual realm, and it is the color of the Ajna chakra, or the chakra associated with the Third Eye. Those with a purple aura are very spiritual and in tune with their psychic abilities. They also tend to have very high levels of intuition. Their Third Eye chakra is very likely fully awakened and very developed and active. Those with a purple aura are likely also very wise.

- **White or Silver** – White and silver are the rarest of aura colors, and are colors of purity. They indicate a close connection to divinity. Those with a white or silver aura have a high level of divine energy and are often very spiritual. It also indicates a higher self. Devout followers of their spirituality are known to have a white or silver aura. This is not to be confused with white spots, however, which are an indication of illness or disease. A true white aura is fully, clearly white with no spots. A white aura can also indicate a woman that is pregnant, or the presence of angels.

- **Dark** – A dark or generally black or gray aura can indicate a negative nature in an individual. It could show you a liar, someone with maleficent intentions, or someone who is deceitful. It can also indicate grief, an inability to forgive, grudges, and negative energy.

- **Bright, Yellow-Gold** – Someone with a bright, yellow-gold aura specifically concentrated around their head is someone who is likely a spiritual leader or teacher. They are also very pure in their intentions and are generally a good person.

Spots

White spots on the etheric layer indicate a health issue that that individual may have. Black spots on the emotional layer indicate maleficent negative energies that manifest themselves as emotions such as sadness or depression. Generally, spots on an aura layer indicate something negative or unhealthy in that person or being, whether it is emotional health, mental health, or physical health.

Size and Range

Those with a large aura that is further from their body are said to have a weaker aura, or that they are easily manipulated and taken advantage of. Those with a smaller aura closer to their bodies are said to have a stronger aura that is not easily shaken.

Chapter 5: Clairvoyance

By definition, clairvoyance is the ability to have a clear vision. In this sense, it would be a clear psychic vision, as we develop clairvoyance through our psychic capabilities. The word clairvoyance is derived from the French language, where claire means clear and voir means to see. So, clairvoyance literally means clear sight!

There are actually six clair senses, but in this chapter, we will focus on clairvoyance. The sister senses, so to speak, are all derived from the same claire root, meaning clear, and have to do with things such as clear smell, hearing, and so forth on a psychic plane. In this chapter, we will be focusing on clear psychic vision. This can show itself to people in visions, communications, or sightings with spirits, imaginary childhood friends, mental images, and much more.

It is often thought that clairvoyance is passed on from generation to generation, but it can be developed by anyone with the dedication to do so. Everyone has the capability, whether big or small, to tap into their clairvoyant abilities.

As briefly stated above, clairvoyance can be present in a spectrum of forms, from seeing loved ones who have died, to viewing what you previously supposed was an imaginary friend as a child, to seeing spirit guides and mental images that are projected upon you through your Ajna. Many psychics and mediums close their eyes when they see images, and that is an example of when they are using their third eye and seeing clearly with their mind. By closing their eyes, they can focus on their vision with much more clarity than if their worldly eyes were open to distractions.

In fact, many mediums and psychics who have mastered this ability have made their living off of it. Most peoples' perceptions of psychics, as they define them, are based on those with clairvoyant abilities. In popular media, psychics can see the future and communicate with spirits. That is clairvoyance and specific abilities that branch off from this clair sense. However, the true nature of this clair sense spans far beyond what we see in media. It is also much deeper and used rarely for show or for only financial gain. What we gain from this sense is pure, enlightening, and personal.

Clairvoyance's Close Link With Our Psychic Perception and the Universe

Psychic perception, and in this specific case clairvoyance, is a timeless well of information. With clairvoyance, you can gain and expand upon a wider scope of information and understanding than with any of the other psychic abilities we will discuss in this book. The psychic sight you gain with clairvoyance cannot be swayed or muddied by the physical world or solid objects, which define and limit how most people sense space, time, and more.

For instance, we grow up thinking that a clock, a physical, tangible object, tells us all we need to know about time. This is not the case. With clairvoyance, we see beyond the tangible and commonplace aspects of ideas like time. We gain a heightened, expansive, clarified view of the universe and beyond when we tap into our clairvoyant sense. There is so much untapped potential in that mind of yours and the world around you that it may even shock you, but do not let it shock you out of believing! If you get too overwhelmed, you may get skeptical. Take caution, however, because skepticism is the fall of psychic awakening and your psychic abilities.

The best way to remedy this is to keep your mind open and not fall to worldly views that people will throw at you. Stay strong, stay open, and stay enlightened! Only then will you truly be able to unlock the full potential of your clairvoyance.

How to Find Your Clairvoyance and Kickstart Your Abilities

In order for clairvoyance to work, so to speak, and to unlock your clairvoyant abilities, you need to delve deep into your Ajna chakra. Meditate, calm yourself, and reach out with your clair sense of sight. Look clearly through your mind's eye, while also looking at clear *spaces*. What I mean by this is that you must look into clear fields of energy and not focus specifically on worldly objects. That is, just reverting back to your physical sight, as clairvoyance reaches far beyond that. It is a heightened, psychic sight through your mind's eye.

You must look past the physical plane by tapping into your mind's eye so you can see further into the psychic realm. That way, you can see energy which is purer, and have a line of sight which is not muddied by the physical world.

Think of these energies like lines; lines that connect objects to their psychic relationships, and counterparts. For instance, within us are our chakras. Each chakra resides in us, but it reaches out as well. Take the root chakra, for example. Your root chakra, or Muladhara, lies at the base of your spine. When you anchor or root yourself, while practicing meditation, you close your eyes and focus your energy into that chakra to root yourself not only to where you are physically resting, but also into the energy of the earth below you. As the root chakra is represented by the color red, imagine your root chakra as a red spinning ball or wheel at the base of your spine. Then, imagine a red line reaching from your spine, like a hand, into the energies of the earth beneath you in order to grasp onto that earthly energy and root you to the ground for stability.

See, you didn't focus on the physical, but instead on the psychic energies of an entity. Another example could be envisioning a white shield of protection around yourself while meditating or cleansing your auras. This mind's visual has a spiritual and very real connection that reaches far past the physical plane. That same idea must be utilized while tapping into your clairvoyant abilities.

Search with your mind's eye for a connection, and for information, that you can truly *feel* at a deep level in your spirit and mind. That is the true essence and utilization of your clairvoyant sense. Urge yourself to be able to look further, to look past the physical, and pick up on that which is subtle to the mortal senses.

Pay particular attention to detail and absorb it, for the *seeing* part of clear seeing goes far beyond one's ability to simply *look*. Anyone can look, but their eyes are dismissive and rove over what they say they see. That's not seeing, and that has absolutely no relation to clarity. Open your eyes, open your Third Eye, and see! Seeing means the ability to understand and deeply perceive what you are viewing with deep thought and strong levels of intuition.

Clairvoyance as it Applies to Other Psychic Development Properties and Practices

Clairvoyance is such a strong and prominent psychic ability that it branches and bleeds into other energy fields and psychic abilities you possess. In reality, everything in the psychic realm, including chakras, and the clair senses, is intertwined intimately as they all revolve around energies. Here are a few examples!

Clairvoyance and Chakras

The more balanced and developed your chakras are, the clearer your clair senses will be. For clairvoyance, try to cleanse and balance your chakras while focusing on and strengthening the Ajna, or Third Eye, chakra. You might like to experiment with Reiki, a specific practice that uses light touch and energy to balance and unlock your chakras. Make sure to find an experienced, trusted practitioner to unblock your energy flows and align your chakras.

Clairvoyance and Meditation

Meditation is also key, for it will help you relax and heighten your sensitivity to what is around you, within you, and beyond you while allowing you to focus more clearly. Meditation will help open up the mind's eye and allow you to develop your clair senses to a sharper point. It will also give you peace and relax your senses, so they are more fluid and flexible. This will give your clairvoyance a lengthier reach. Additionally, it can rid your chakra of negative or chaotic energy that could mar your abilities and stem your psychic energy. Meditation also improves your short-term memory. With meditation, you will be able to retain what you see so you can deepen your understanding of the visions you receive with your clairvoyant abilities.

Clairvoyance and Auras

For extra practice, you can also try sensing auras, as this develops your mind's eye and your clairvoyant capabilities. Aura reading is actually a branch of clairvoyance, as you must see beyond the physical into the deeper sight of energies and psychic meaning. Clairvoyance and auras have a similarity like squares and rectangles. Just as a square is a rectangle while a rectangle is not a square, auras are a type of clairvoyant ability while clairvoyance is not solely defined by aura viewing. Therefore, practicing aura viewing is a great way to dip your feet into clairvoyant abilities. It is a great first step, and it is not difficult to do. Soon you will see the world clearly in a new light and with technicolor vision!

Chapter 6: Telepathy

By definition, telepathy is the transmission of information between two sentient beings by means of extrasensory communication. In other words, it is the ability to read, understand, transmit, and receive thoughts, images, words, and other means from one person or being to another through psychic channels and not physical capacities.

The word telepathy actually has Greek roots. Tele, in Greek, means distance. Pathos, the root of the last half of the word telepathy, means either feeling, perception, passion, or experience, all of which apply in varying ways to one's telepathic abilities.

The Different Forms of Telepathy

Telepathy, contrary to popular belief, is not simply the act of reading someone's mind and thoughts. One can, in certain cases, read someone's mind, but telepathy reaches far beyond that. There are five types of telepathy that we will discuss in this chapter, as they are the most universally accepted in the psychic community. We will go over each one of those in detail now.

Latent Telepathy (Formerly Known as Deferred Telepathy)

With latent telepathy, there is almost always a delay in time between the information being sent out from a being and when it is received by one with the telepathic skill. This time lag may cause a bit of confusion, but with the strength of your intuition, it will become clearer with time. When the entity from which the telepathy is transmitted sends out their message, the recipient may not be aware of it for a span of time, but it will come.

Retrocognitive, Precognitive, and Intuitive Telepathy

Retrocognitive, precognitive, and intuitive telepathy are much like the psychic abilities of retrocognition, precognition, and intuition we touched on in the first few chapters of this book. I have lumped them together here because they are all the same, with the exception of one difference: Time. With these forms of telepathy, one receives information that has been transferred from different time periods or states of mind. What this means is that the informational transfer is linked to either the past, the present, or the future state of a sentient being's mind to the receiver, or the person who has this retrocognitive telepathic ability. The receiver is in the present time, but the telepathic messages this person receives can be from many different points in time. The use of intuition is key here for determining the time period from which these messages came. With the use of your

Third Eye's guidance, spirit guides, and deduction from the information received, you can gain a clearer understanding of these messages and the party from whom you receive them.

Emotive Telepathy (Also Known as Remote Influence or Emotional Transfer)

Emotive telepathy has less to do with specific information or thoughts and more to do with the transmissions of emotions or sensations themselves. They are often in altered states, but the person with this ability can feel or sense emotions, feelings, or other sensations transmitted from another sentient being such as a family member, friend, or even a stranger. With this form of telepathy, there is a much more tangible feeling involved. Emotive telepathy is very intimate in nature and can either be beneficial or harmful, depending on whether the feelings involved are positive or negative in nature. This form of telepathy has a direct effect on your body and mind, so it is felt at a much deeper level than the other forms of telepathy discussed here. The emotions are directly transferred from an entity to the telepathic receiver, and they are felt very strongly.

Dream Telepathy

Dream telepathy is exactly what it sounds like: Telepathy received through dreams. It is the ability to step into someone else's dreamscape, or for another person to step into yours, to transmit messages, images, ideas, and more. It has been linked closely to lucid dreaming, but it is a bit different and much deeper than basic lucid dreaming. If anything, it is a deeper and more developed form of lucid dreaming. Dream telepathy is often incredibly vivid, seemingly random, yet very true. When you wake up from dream telepathy, you often vividly remember the details and find them to be true.

Superconscious Telepathy

This form of telepathy is greatly enlightened and on par with a higher level of knowledge and awakening than the others. This form of telepathy is said to be shared among all species as a collective mind and a collective well of information and insight. With this ability, you can tap into and access the wisdom of the world and the human species as a whole. This is a very advanced form of telepathy that has to do with the collective unconscious of the universe, through which you unlock profound knowledge and understanding.

How to Develop Your Telepathy

Communication of the mind is very difficult if you do not know how to recognize it, develop it, and strengthen it. First of all, you must keep an open mind. The mind's eye is critical in this psychic ability, for it is through which you will receive the telepathically transmitted information. If it is shut off, closed, or barred in any way, telepathy will be nearly impossible.

Therefore, you must connect with your Third Eye chakra or your Ajna. Focus on it and strengthen it. Awaken your mind's eye to unlock these abilities and gain a full, heightened outlet of knowledge. Meditate and center yourself. Create balance in your chakras and open your mind. Reach out with your Third Eye and with your Ajna chakra energies, and you may be surprised with what you discover.

Now, we all possess the gift of telepathy if we just take the time to find and develop it. You have to throw away the skepticism that the world has wrapped around this ability; for if you do not, you will never be able to experience this great psychic ability. Telepathy is natural and very real, and you have to believe that moving forward. With that said, let's go over just how we can develop this ability.

The biggest step one should take when developing their telepathy is to strengthen their intuitive abilities. We touched on this in the chapter on the Third Eye, but just as it applied in that chapter, it applies here. As a first step, open your mind. Allow it to dream and imagine, which are wonderful ways to bolster your mind and your psyche. Get creative in whatever way comes naturally to you. Write out your thoughts and your feelings, paint, draw, sing, create music, stories, and ideas! Open yourself up to wonderful possibilities. Then, reflect, think, and seek to understand the messages behind your creations. Open up your eyes and your mind to the meanings behind what you have created, for that is your subconscious talking to you. It goes hand in hand with the psychic realm. It is interconnected with the energies that you will be transmitting and receiving messages from. Unlock your intuition and your potential, and you will be well on your way to opening your telepathic pathways.

Lucid dreaming is another wonderful way to develop your telepathic capacity as well as your intuition and your Third Eye, which, as I have said, is critical to utilizing and strengthening your telepathy. Lucid dreaming is vivid; it can be controlled by you, experienced by you, and flood you with insight and information about your subconscious and your true abilities.

Next, remove yourself from your physical body. Focus on your inner spirit and your third eye. This out of body experience is exactly the feeling you will need in order to communicate telepathically, as your spirit and mind travel to transmit and receive this telepathic information. By separating yourself from your body and all worldly distractions, you can turn your attention to your thoughts, perceptions, and nonphysical senses.

Find a partner with whom you are comfortable with to practice this ability. You should both start by meditating in order to calm your minds, align your chakras, and focus on what is about to occur. This is a good place to start in order to prepare yourselves to send and receive messages. Next, each should sit far away from each other in the same room, but facing each other. Decide who will transmit and who will receive. If you are the transmitter, which is best in this practice, close your eyes and create a detailed idea of the message you will be sending. Then, picture the partner with which you are working, clearly. Now, send your message. Visualize it leaving your mind and traveling to your partner, who will receive it. Then stop, meditate, and repeat if they did not receive it.

Once you are through, have your partner take out a piece of paper and a writing utensil and let them write down the details of what their perception of the transmission was. Compare this to what you sent to your partner, then keep practicing until what they write is similar to what you sent.

Finally, be patient. Have an open mind and do not get discouraged. This will take time, dedication, and practice. Nobody can develop this ability in just a few minutes. You will slowly and naturally progress and improve over time. You do not want to strain your abilities and block your chakra energies, or it could harm you and hinder your psychic abilities. Be calm, be patient, and it will come.

Chapter 7: How to Develop the Different Psychic Abilities

The most critical component of your higher level of consciousness, once your Third Eye is awakened, is the understanding, developing, and honing of your psychic abilities as a whole. Psychic abilities have a very wide range and incorporate a substantial amount of energy, chakra strength, Third Eye awakening, and more. Here, I will discuss basic techniques that will allow you to hone and strengthen any psychic abilities you choose to pursue, as well as things that could harm your abilities' development or halt it completely. As we have discussed the most prominent and popular psychic abilities for beginners in the past chapters, this will be a general overview of psychic abilities as a whole and how we can strengthen them and apply good practices to our spiritual lives.

Psychic Abilities and Skepticism

Let us start out with the bad so we can end on a good note. In the psychic community, and for your own personal health, the greatest demise of psychic abilities is the introduction of skepticism. Psychic abilities, and the Third Eye, revolve around one's attunement to intuition and an open mind. Skepticism brings failure to one's ability to hone their psychic abilities and embody a truly open mind. Skeptics ask too many questions, doubt the reality of psychic energy, and try to debunk the psychic realm. This is a maleficent force that hinders the true acceptance and very essence of a person's psychic abilities. Thoughts such as "Why am I doing this?" or, "Is this *really* going to work?", or "Am I really seeing this, or am I crazy?" hinder your Third Eye more than you know. Instead of saying, "Am I really seeing this, or is it all in my head?" realize that it is in your head, but in the best way. Your mind is open; you are absorbing and experiencing so many new things. Revel in this! Let it bring you joy and wonder, not the feeling of being overwhelmed or a negatively questioning mind. Embody the reality of the psychic mindset. Then, and only then, can you unlock your psychic abilities.

Now, onto the positives.

The Importance of Meditation

Now, I know I have gone over this point a number of times in this book, but that is because it is infinitely important for every single psychic ability and your health as a whole. When you meditate, you have the potential to tap into each one of your chakras, unlocking their energy so that it can flow beautifully. Many psychic abilities target specific chakras. Practicing meditation, so you learn how to focus your chakra energies is critically important for you to be able to tap into those energies when the time comes. We've already talked about the Third Eye chakra, but your root chakra is also very important when it comes to meditation. This chakra can help you create an anchor for you to hold on to for stability when utilizing any psychic ability. Close your eyes and envision the base of your spine. Focus on that chakra energy, a vortex or spinning wheel anchoring to the very place on which you sit. Now, envision a red line that reaches beneath you into the very core of the earth. This will anchor you, stabilize you, and give you an incredible sense of balance that is important for balancing your chakras as a whole and giving you peace of mind, body, emotions, and spirit. This control and strength will benefit you in unimaginable ways throughout your journey with all psychic abilities.

Intuition Is the Gateway Into Psychic Strength

Intuition stems from the mind's eye and the Ajna chakra, and it fuels our capability to tap into the psychic plane around and within us. Keep your mind open; find details in every little thing, explore, experience, create, imagine! There are so many ways to develop your keen intuition skills, and they will all positively boost your psychic abilities. The imagination is a vivid, beautiful thing that opens our minds to unnatural possibilities and outcomes that could be very real if you know how to read them properly! Intuition is thoroughly saturated with energies from your mind, and that saturation can bleed into your mind's eye in a good way if you let loose and let it in!

Balance Your Chakras

Chakras are the base of all of our energy and link us to the energies in the world and beyond. By balancing and unblocking your chakras, you will unleash the highest levels of flow and control that you can achieve with your psychic energy. You can do this with meditation, a guide, or through therapeutic means like Reiki. Chakras link very intimately with your psychic abilities, mind, body, emotions, and energies as a whole, so balancing them is a very important step. Balance is the natural way of the universe, and it paves the way for clarity, peace, knowledge, understanding, and vision.

Use Your Clairvoyance to Call Out to Your Spirit Guide or Guides

This may seem a bit advanced, but if you have developed your clairvoyance enough to identify your spirit guides, they will give you the wisdom and guidance you require in order to fully awaken and develop your psychic abilities. These come in many forms, from animals, to people, to simply voices and sounds that guide you in big or small ways. Spirit guides can also be angels or loved ones who have passed. They can bridge the spiritual realm and reach out to you in aid. They are also known as soul mentors, as they can help you strengthen and heal your spirit and find peace. Call upon these spirit guides for support, strength, guidance, clarity, and more so that they can teach you how to develop your psychic abilities to their greatest potential! Calling out to them and identifying them will also help you develop your sense of clairvoyance and discover how in sync you are with your Third Eye chakra or Ajna.

Did you know that you can also request a specific sign or guide? For instance, if you are really struggling with a decision and your mind is going in a million different directions, anchor and center yourself with your root chakra and focus on a specific image or entity you would like to see that may guide you along your path.

Practice, Practice, and Practice Again!

Take care not to tire yourself out, as that can negatively impact your abilities and drain your energy, but practice your abilities, meditation, and balancing your chakras to unlock the full potential of your psychic abilities! The easiest things to practice, in the beginning, are meditation and aura reading, but once you get more comfortable with your other abilities, branch out and practice those as well for a well-rounded level of psychic development. You can also practice predicting certain outcomes, then when the time comes to pass, see how accurate your foretelling abilities are. I simply ask that you practice whenever you are able to, and practice with an open mind and a full heart. This will help you become the psychic individual you were meant to be!

Conclusion

I sincerely thank you with all of the gratitude in my heart chakra for reading this book to completion. I hope that this book has informed you to your very core and has helped you zero in on the importance of the psychic world and its special abilities. If you truly take these words to heart, I know you can experience and accomplish great things. Just listen to your mind's eye, your senses, and that which surrounds you, and you will be well on your way to enlightening your mind, body, spirit, and emotions.

Next, I urge you to apply what you have learned in this book so you can flourish in life! Take these practices and make them your own. Hone your psychic abilities, so you can leap forward and reach your full psychic potential!

In this book, we have discussed many of the psychic abilities that can present themselves to us throughout our lives. This includes the six clair senses, the ability to foresee and remember events and connect them together as one, the ability to view and understand auras, how to understand and develop telepathy, and much more! We went through what the Third Eye is, how to awaken it, and how to apply it to the other abilities. We learned what the seven chakras are and how they move energy throughout our bodies like spinning wheels, and we learned what each chakra represents and where it resides in our bodies. Then, we discussed how to practice, develop, hone, and protect our psychic abilities through meditation, pushing away skepticism, focused determination, and more. I will leave you with this final piece of advice: Never lose sight of who you are, what you can do, and what you can become.

Again, I thank you for choosing this book from all of the similar guides on the market today. I sincerely hope that you have not been disappointed, but rather, awakened! I appreciate your interest in this book, and I wish you the best on your journey into the psychic realm!

www.ingramcontent.com/pod-product-compliance
Lightning Source LLC
LaVergne TN
LVHW011740060526
838200LV00051B/3265